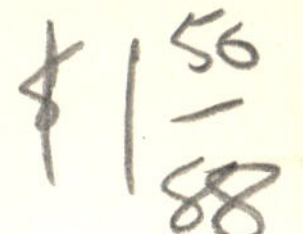

$1 \frac{56}{88}$

$ 3.00

AF411910

EVIDENCE OF FASCISM IN GREECE
STORIES BY JUDITH GROSSMAN
POURBOIRE PRESS 1975

Frieze was first published as a pamphlet from Burning Deck.

Some of these stories first appeared in *The Providence Review.*

Special thanks to:
Michael Gizzi, Bruce Macpherson, Jaimy Gordon

Cover by Keith Waldrop

LC 75-24939
ISBN 0-915176-09-2

P. O. Box 315, Woods Hole, Mass. 02543
Peter Kaplan, Editor

For Michael Lynch

TABLE OF CONTENTS

EVIDENCE OF FASCISM IN GREECE

for Alice Pitkin

First the ensemble—a rousing of tavern sitters, shirking shepherds, jointless, tripping over country women, gape-toothed and waddling, teen-age truants, ragbound orphans, limping, cane-stricken whining elders, losing focus, wobbling, field mice under boards gnawing, tweezer wielding, grinning, lice abounding.

Do they meet in the evening to rehearse   line up for paychecks   in the evening to rehearse   for another week of screams for paychecks   to be beaten into another week?

Compressed under garbage can covers, arms proffer tickets. Throats chill in dark alleys, not to the frost of a blade or pistol, but to the moist frayed edge of an unsold sweepstakes ticket. Through a sewer grating, finger and thumb disclose a slender slip of ticket. And delivered from the bills of low-flying birds ...

They take their training together, then scatter. Installed into uniform, they assume location. In the morning, street signals flare up like screams — banks of fire — from corner to corner.

Joseph the alcoholic is singing. He straddles a path adjacent to the caves above the sea. His overcoat trips him, so slowly, that at least one dweller on each level tries to touch him as he falls. Deposits of glass break from his pockets, shining—due to the influence of the moon—red as resin, the depth of brandy. We hear him singing.

Small bands of sellers strain for coherence — enunciate in rumbles, waves, stay aloft in unison, emit mumbles in waves, sway back and forth — their passage felt as jolts under the sidewalk. Pedestrians conform to the rhythm.

A woman with plate and spoon emerges from the field. Noticing the pack on his back, her gesture and expression combine grief. With one hand she measures the bulk of his burden, with the other she offers the plate — berries rife with sugar. He moves backwards, mouthing, "No it is not heavy, No I am not hungry," mouthing, because they do not know each other's sounds. She smiles and speaks, smiles and speaks. "She knows me only as a spice merchant, bankrupt, astray from the trade routes, she is searching for that memory," "unload the pack, peddle rugs, icons, hair or bones for luck, present a letter from a friend twenty years dead." With one hand she lifts the spoon from the plate, with the other she loosens his jaws. She forcefeeds the stranger who has never learned to speak.

Yards later he spits it all out, looks back; she is smiling, speaking, smiling and speaking, holding a plate—empty—and a spoon.

Four or five ticketsellers settle on each corner. Days pass; tickets linger, save a few secure for friends, engaged to stroll by. At random, sellers turn against the crowd, aim: sleeves, elbows, wrists — a threat of nightmare, blood. The street becomes a shell aware of echo; consumers run. Sick with screams, a merchant laments supply and demand — strewn from balance on the sidewalk.

Paratroopers initial *Olympus,* skywriters dominate the sky — *Sparta:* recaptured, *Mycenae,* the tomb of Agamemnon: recaptured, the windmills of *Mykonos:* recaptured, the great canal of *Korinth:* recaptured,

"They litter the streets, a sound formation despite the claque of sneers;
. . . all have found careers, draw income
. . . megaphones, allotted breath breaks, inflatable chairs
. . . limbs, stilts, hooks to trap the passing shoulder, no more donkeys or dirt roads."

TEMPLE SEQUENCE

—Nothing was as it had first appeared.

Guardians of the Silent Garden

Enter the garden of pure pattern. Pay no attention to the signs: *Keep Off The Grass.* No one walks here now but you and I. The soil sustains an even keel. It yields nothing but surface — petals, arranged fossils, wells, roofless ruins. The ruts of footsteps have healed and closed. How restful to gaze upon such stillness. Even fissures in the rocks emit no whispers. Wind is fielded to another locale by concerted effort of all local terrestrial life. Evolution has been restricted to the plant kingdom; precocious species are exported at sheer profit. Proceeds revert to the guardian for maintenance of these sacred grounds.

A Building with a Belfry

Ever since compulsory temple attendance came to its premature end, the building has been deserted. A guardian continues to tidy the plots and snip the foliage planted by the prophets of the order. Rotating shifts of sextons keep the bells ringing on the hour and impose the same severe penalties for ringers found sleeping between midnight and dawn. The community once served by the temple has slowly migrated. Now one hearer must be assigned each ringer that negligence on night duty not be ignored.

Fund Raising

Other sources of funding are one. A dance around the circumference of the gates is held once every templar year. (Temple astrologers divine a stellar calendar which corresponds only incidentally to exterior equivalents.) Dances are not staggered at equal intervals. Sometimes they occur one night after another until the participants, generally drawn from the same lapsed members of the order, near collapse. Then no dances are scheduled — due to fluctuations in the order calendar — for epochs or at least eras. Eventually new generations convene for a similar rotation of marathon and lethargy. When the dancing is frenzied, the bells can be oiled, the gardens be irrigated, the casks be replenished with wine. When the calendar dictates a cessation of such movement, only a murmur indicates a presence in the belfry. The pelting of dust resumes upon the temple and its grounds. Such is the interdependence of astrology and dance within this economic system. Such is the symbiosis of treads, time, tonality and mirth.

Miracles

Miracles invade this community by a somewhat parallel scheme. But the order exerts as little influence upon variety as upon frequency of these spontaneous acts. Veterans are bored by the standard repertoire. They are wary of bloodstained garments, wounds inflicted by no apparent agent, floods emanating from statues, talking idols. Cures effected by prayer are often worse than the original ailment. They reject the majority of their visions, would like to revise the common revelations. "Why do our miracles lack humor?" they cry to the ceilings of their barren dwellings. The pacing is monotonous, the outcome predictable, the oracles self-composed and smug. Maybe a plague could be interspersed among the miracles.

Famine

Famine and fast are often indistinguishable, one from another. Famines are almost frowned upon as a dangerous absence of temptation. Almost always famines occur in quick succession. Plenties vary, but seldom cater to the consumer; ice cream is not an ideal food for breaking fast or famine. Prayers of thanks are often begrudged but continue to be offered up.

Night Music

First the ache of wooden planks, fists pummeling the walls, now a cadence sustained by tom cats, a long run of cockroaches through the aisles, then the ping of stained glass, the clean melodic line of clerestory windows, finally the slaking of thirst, the wheeze of altar flames, the dry rustle of pages turned over and over ... all this comes forth in the darkness, never to be uttered twice in the same manner.

The Body is the Temple of the Spirit,

especially the mind which can store up, order, reject and refine all around the fourteen stations, each image absorbed by the eye as the body brushes past one station to the next until the last excursion, the last reply returns to the first and the mind becomes instead a prayer wheel calling forth its own bells until they too, in turn, form a circle of echoes through the hours of the day and the slow watches of the night until, at last, under the plane tree where one decides to seek some rest, the eyes close and the mind puts the body through its paces, the body the mind, and the spirit fragrant with dust is almost all that remains.

Each monk becomes then a miniature temple, identical to the rest, who can convey this structure out of its model into the open air, through the paths he walks, to the people he greets along the way.

Incidental Music

Two brothers relax beneath a tree, arranging duets in the late afternoon. They tune their instruments, one lute, one piccolo, to each others' pitch, then proceed amid scattered bursts of conversation: "But, Cyrus. . ." "Yet, Benjamin. . ."

They revel in contradiction. Conflict is sanctioned if not concerned with fixed doctrine, if not aired in public places.

No prosperous members have joined the order for decades. Offerings have declined at the collect for the past eight fiscal years. Benjamin balances the order budget only by astute juggling of the assets and liabilities columns. He vastly overestimates, for instance, the value of relics sealed within the vaults and coffers of the temple walls. Some of these claimed assets have decayed and disintegrated into fine silt, but Benjamin checks them only at night, hoping faith will restore them by the morning.

Appetites are increasing although production is drastically slow. Scholars, excused from manual duties, devour the scant surplus of both natural and man-made goods brought forth by the remaining laborers. Cyrus defends these thinkers, "Meditation is the bloodstream of any order," "Deprive the mystics of nourishment and we all perish alike." Benjamin holds fast to the dignity of labor, "External achievement should not be shunned. The spiritual pursues the material as much as the material craves the spiritual sphere."

They fall into dissonance, producing loud blatant solos, friction visible in the bright afternoon air. Still, it is good in the shade with the music and the tunes and some water to quench an occasional thirst. They fall asleep upon each other's shoulders as the bells imitate the melody they initiated hours before.

In the Refectory

Discipline has collapsed at community meals. High etiquette — suitable for ceremonial feasts, seasonal banquets, for the paying of respects to visiting dignitaries — is rebuked and forgotten. Low etiquette — adequate for simple fare, basic suppers, dry toast and tea — is seldom observed. Grace has been dropped as a formality before the partaking of nourishment.

The monks dine upon long trestle tables, heads bent close to their laden plates. When one member of the order lets slip a particle of food, others crawl under the table to compete for the scraps. Scuffling ensues; one brother emerges with minor scratches, tufts of hair uprooted about his ears, clothes rumpled and disarranged, knees scraped, hands soiled from dust collecting on the floor. Disengaged diners continue undisturbed, alternating fork and spoon at convenient intervals. No one is punished: neither the yielders to temptation nor the apparent cause of the tempting action—the awkward diner whose slip, however minor, threw his brothers into open combat.

Bread is broken into unequal portions, leading to demands for uniformly sliced loaves. Water is devoid of blessing, drained from the pitcher, sipped from goblets before a hand can sanction the contents. Wine has been wholly omitted from the menu due to feuds erupting before, during and after consumption. But a brother can bring his choice of beverage at his own discretion and risk.

And so the monks slouch upon the low concrete benches, having relaxed the upright posture that once contributed to their fame. They elbow their neighbors on either side, kick each other beneath the table without shifting facial expression, find communion only in mutual complaint: the benches are uncomfortable, impractically designed for human anatomy, even that constrained within a spiritual frame; the meals are unbalanced, consisting mainly of starch, carbohydrates and local produce picked from the herb and vegetable garden — scarce now that the afternoon nap has become an established right. Consecration no longer blinds them to the blandness of their bread, the monotone pattern of sleeping and waking, the lack of surprises in repeated prayer.

Now even their muscles mutiny beneath their uniform robes — sweltering in summer, frozen stiff in winter, abrasive to the texture of the skin, trailing just enough material to trip them several times a day... Coming and going is no longer conducted in common; any given brother begins the meal whenever he elects and continues at his own pace. No excuses are forthcoming when a brother leaves the trestle table, the low concrete bench.

Program Music

Some monks approach, making their slow shuffle up the long central aisle of the building. Coffins grow heavier and heavier as members of the order decline, leaving few to assist in conducting the mortal burden towards its final rites. Necessary duties must be performed with the meagre personnel and resources left the community; heavily embroidered robes, torchlight processions, contrapuntal musical offerings have been stored up and put away with other memories of the past. Sharing of functions has become severe since the death of the official organist; one bearer must desert the cortege from time to time to play a few stops on the organ, then hurry down the balcony stairs to resume the carrying of the coffin.

Their music is plain, consisting of straight melodic lines, some hums, refrains, chants, phrasing altered at whim by individual singers; the tunes are familiar and well memorized. Singers emit only melody; their music predates the discovery of harmony (a technique they pretend to ignore or are, perhaps, physically incapable of producing). The instrumentalists — strummers of the lute, violists de gamba, continuo players, oboists, flautists, trumpeters, and drummers — have disappeared along with the choir and official organist. The acappella effect of the present ensemble rebounds with a nasal echo left lingering in the temple and over its grounds, as if a pedal were depressed on the piano long after the fingers had been lifted from the keyboard.

The pace of the procession has slowed down to a drone, to the tempo of the melody proclaimed. Soon no one will arise to perform the ceremony, but merely to participate directly in the funeral rites. The remaining monks register each face in the file, counting their ranks with alarm. Who will be the last to linger? Each has set aside enough strength to perform singlehandedly the rites and ablutions, to take up residence in the temporary resting place. But who will then transfer the last occupant from his place upon the altar to his final resting place in the communal order graveyard?

Lapses and Prefabrications

Subsequently, temple time is not strictly adhered to. Atemplar time begins to govern certain events, select movements. Bells mourn the loss of reliable ringers; volunteers do not come forth to relieve the silent hours. Ritual fasting goes unobserved even during famines. Dancing sets its own pace: Commence whenever partners fancy!

New residents are settling in the vicinity. They demand a new temple building although they would preserve the ancient belfry. The building is demolished; the belfry remains, suspended in the sky — one sacristan within. For the newcomers a revelation, for the natives an innovative miracle, perhaps the last. A prefabricated temple minus optional belfry is slid gently under the ancient tower.

THE PEACOCK ROOM

". . . Tragedy lurks about the Peacock Room, too."

Freer Gallery of Art, Washington, D.C.
Publication 4024 (Rev.), 1965.

I
Prelude and Description

I settled upon it my skill, my vision, and my sense of color. During the period of gestation, I never left its gilded walls.

At night I took excursions into the interior,

> The room is endless; it cannot
> be exhausted by the pacing of
> a lifetime. I am hampered by
> the need to paint, polish, and
> upholster every surface that
> I pass.

I awoke each morning far from rested — teeth chattering, limbs sore, muscle disconnected — not at all poised for maximum efficiency. Claw marks ravaged the careful design of the walls.

So half of each day was spent undoing the mistakes of the previous evening. But the windowless room still lured me toward its problems of completion.

I became as soundless as a peacock scuttling first the width, then the length of the room.

II
Guests

Callers came upon me as I worked. Some strode in early dressed in formal garb. The men wore frock coats and suspenders. Heavy watch fobs dangled from their chests. One military figure carefully perfected the outline of his moustache with the curved blade of a long saber. Under his chin he propped a tiny silver moustache cup bearing his initials. Aides de camp inserted monocles to witness the spectacle.

Most gentlemen escorted one or two women tucked

under each arm. The ladies, veils upon their eyes, slouched in long brocade dresses. Semi-precious stones glittered on their wrists. Ostrich feathers encircled their heads. Their presence was a distraction and a hindrance to my concentration.

They spun parasols around and around until the spokes collapsed and deflated the silk coverings. Opening a parasol inside a residence can only lure bad luck and I, surrounded by the unlucky symbol of the peacock, could sustain no further handicap.

They prattled to lap dogs, instructed hounds on leashes—silent at their heels, squealed at the scratches of siamese kittens, rustled cages of pale mice, salamanders and parrots. The kept birds shrieked at the painted peacocks or at their own reflected contours, subdued only by the draping of white sheets over their bars.

Other women, alone, plucked at their eyebrows in hand-held mirrors while their chauffeurs dozed in the dark interiors of carriages halted outside.

Later in the evening, visitors lingered in loose careless tunics, untied shoelaces and shapeless hats: sleepwalkers I turned in another direction. Bohemians, idlers, passersby, blind and ailing strollers met under the aegis of my room.

Artists personally drained bottles brought for communal celebration. Often they collapsed while competing for a vantage point from which to steal trade secrets. A painter from my former circle protruded a hand from the center of a pallette stuck upon his elbow, in an appeal both for medical aid and a position as my apprentice.

The house became an object of conjecture to the outside world, a source of severe anguish to my patron. Rumors circulated of its function as brothel, gambling parlor, a site for the staging of secret, illegal duels, an agency for the procurement of absinthe, laudanum and other forbidden essences, a shelter for radical societies.

None of these rumors were unfounded. Keepers of the peace were absorbed into violent covenants. Reunions of revolutionary sects occurred by chance.

Elder sages from the first Paris Commune (1792-1794) consoled the veterans of 1848. Newly liberated survivors of the second Paris Commune (March, 1871-May, 1871) recounted their heroic struggles.

Friction was renewed between rival factions of this historical panorama. One comrade of 1848 elbowed a syndicalist bystander. Another prodded a libertarian with the pointed edge of his placard – *Capitalism Cripples!* Followers of Kropotkin resisted the fierce demeanor of Bakuninists marshalled in another corner.

Ladies slipped under the protection of arms not always identical to those under which they had first emerged. Refreshment vendors proffered mysterious tea-time treats. Dice were found far flung from the hands of their original owners.

I greeted them all in the doorway. They offered tidbits. I refused. They pried into the decor of the room. I obstructed their view with contortions of my arms and fingers. They prompted me to speak. I drew my lips into my mouth. Finally they tickled me. I broke the silence of the room with the squall of the peacock — uttered only in moments of extreme terror, a sound too acute for perception by the outer ear, but reeling to the nervous system and inner centers of balance. The guest list diminished year by year.

III
Painting and Patronage

At selected intervals, the patron would conduct surprise inspections. In the beginning of our association, he was a constant presence, but he had since grown old and exasperated. "This room was intended as my place of retirement, not your life work," he had announced. "You should be paying rent, not collecting a fee."

Each time the patron appeared, he approved the room less and less. I would make the necessary changes and he would return. But the Spanish leather covering the walls had become so thick, the gilt pattern upon the leather so massive, that he could no longer detect improvements.

I had painted the patron and myself into the murals lining the room. They had become a chronicle of our collaboration throughout the years.

Our features had faded into the foreground of the early friezes circling the base of the walls. Enamel cracked over the outline of the original scene.

Yet the patron could still be glimpsed, the golden highlights of his hair somewhat mellowed, the rosy tinge of his cheeks subdued. He expressed delight as I plaited his hair with flowers.

By the next frame to the right, however, his likeness had become almost perverse, in an effort to convey the venting of his fury. But the object of his wrath had been deleted from the landscape.

With each gradation of color and tone, with the stain applied to each new stencil — the ingredients of one mural binding those of its successor — the motifs grew darker in design. Deaths were mourned. All callers at the door stood muted in funeral dress. The peacocks were congested in their pens. They could not be coaxed into a display of colors.

I began to labor after nightfall in order to simulate the atmosphere of the room's eventual usage. First I fed the kerosene torches, snipped the wicks, secured the flame within the glass, refueled the gaslights, then stationed hurricane lamps here and there about the room for heightened illumination. Then I would review the murals, friezes, and other decorations as might an eventual visitor to this salon.

The designs must be festive but restrained, suited to the witness of high officials of state, papal representatives, and perhaps, even monarchs.

However, this shifting of light and darkness began to affect my senses. I would neglect to extinguish the lamps, then fail to remember if it were day or night, time to initiate or to bring to a close my daily tasks. I sought respite in daydreams, falling from my stepladder, sliding on the polished floor.

I began to fear ascension of the ladder, unable to predict the time or means of an eventual descent. I began to dread my perch on the scaffold, a feat of balance crucial to the intricate demands of the upper mouldings, a feat now beyond the range of my reflexes.

IV
The Artist at Home

After my dismissal as chief designer, I was removed temporarily to this private chamber, some distance from the site of my former efforts. Here I pass the time rearranging the furniture, polishing my bed frame, and sanding the uneven surface of the floors. I lament the following:

> 1) An inventory discloses only
>   four articles of furniture on
>   the premises:
>   a) a bed
>   b) a table
>   c) a lamp
>   d) a mirror on a stand
> 2) Three of these four objects
>   are glued to the floor. Is
>   this a ship or an asylum?
> 3) Having accepted these givens,
>   I find the possible combina-
>   tions and recombinations of
>   factors towards the recon-
>   struction of this room to be
>   severely limited.
> 4) The aforementioned furnish-
>   ings are not only sparse and
>   immobile, but composed of
>   inferior materials.

Only once have I glimpsed the Peacock Room since deportation to this new address. To my horror, I found it utterly changed. Another artist or architect, an imposter to those titles, had marred my Spanish leather, taken a scissors to my tapestries, and vandalized my murals and friezes in order to complement the perspective of his own paintings, now displayed prominently in that room.

I have not forgotten my personal investment of time and energy in the interests of the patron's project. This morning while combing my hair before the mirror, I noted the glint of gold flakes still imbedded in my eyelashes from that era.

I plan to petition for reentrance to the Peacock Room, for reinstatement in my previous position. In the meantime, I formulate plans of great complexity.

THE NOTEBOOK

I

The notebook disturbed the arrangement of the museum sales counter. It bore no resemblance to Tutankhamen's baby bracelet. It could not be mistaken for a calendar or for a lifetime membership plaque. It benefitted no charity. Nor had it reproduced. It was an original. Itself.

The cover of the notebook was now without a mark of its initial color. Air and light had settled brown, grey and green upon its surface.

Inside the cover a name instantly recognizable as a minor but still significant artist of the early nineteenth century was inscribed, along with a date — eighteen forty-seven.

On the following pages, the name was subjected to various gyrations of calligraphy and mediums: on one page printed in crayon, each letter separate and distinct; on another page blended into an impression by pastel chalk. Slowly, version by version, it assumed almost the color of the page—a shadow, a watermark.

Various titles, preceding and following the name, also appeared throughout the notebook indicating changes in sex, profession, levels of noble and, at times, royal status.

The spaces surrounding the transformations of the name were filled with caricatures, isolated aspects of the face and of the body, miniature landscapes, geometric formations and a sequence of notes.

> Some absent-minded collector had relinquished the notebook — from a pocket, from a hand, from a mind forever. But the trace of mildew clinging to parts of his clothing, the musty odor persisting in certain regions of his rooms will eventually draw him back to the source.
>
> or
>
> A highly emotional owner of the notebook — perhaps connected by blood or by affection to the first owner — had severed himself from it, knowing he was no longer capable or worthy of its possession. He placed the notebook on the counter as one might place a child on the steps of an orphanage.

II

A massive swerving of peoples can be detected in the vicinity of the museum. The facade of the building is no longer apparent. Policemen, braced for the possible lunge of a rebel, tend a semblance of lines. In the struggle to preserve a place in line, some spectators have established residence in the surrounding streets.

Only by chance does a follower of the notebook approach me in conversation:

Some time ago, he explains, the notebook began spontaneously to issue ink from its binding.

Linotype operators, private investigators and a medieval order of Irish scribes have selected it as an object of veneration.

Scoffers, however, contend that a squid survives some depths below the present site of the notebook. Persecuted by the tramplings of the crowd, he caused a complete outpouring of his ink. The ink, having surfaced through the floor as a protest, was mistaken on arrival for a blessing.

Most of those gathered here are not attentive to the notebook or its powers. Instead they survey the notions of the crowd; pausing at intervals to focus on one another.

Casting a glance of sympathy for the follower's position, I withdraw. Memories of flipping pages, pencilling comments in the margins, even folding down corners for future reference remain suppressed, as will the boast of a set of initials, deeply etched into the soft front cover of the notebook.

FRIEZE

Two girls lean from the window out into the street. One, his cousin, scans the city for a suitor, promised to return for just one day. The other, a friend, watches as well, in a dress of complimentary color.

To spectators below, they appear as regular as night blooming flowers. Children point them out as crepe paper banners, recast into dye each evening, then flung out to dry.

In strolls the doctor. The elevator opens, reveals him, he is seated. He annexes chairs — in their midst he will reside for the morning, afternoon or evening of his visit.

Perpendicular to the doctor paces his mother. A man and woman who, if removed, would appear to be attending a ping pong tournament, follow her back and forth movement.

Guests loiter in the doorway, waiting their turn to arrive. They fret away the time by locating, among the available options, the particular tableau in which they thrive. (They litter the carpet with shreds of invitations. They aim spitballs at the tapestries. They threaten to organize. They seem pacified by four o'clock tea.) Some favor the window, others the circle of chairs; the remainder ape the mother's pace. New guests are invited on the average of one every clockwise; none will be received.

Children play beneath the colors in the window until called away. "In that house, a party is always going on," they convince one another.

Synopsis

Conflict, in contrast to *infatuation* (in this household —
cyclical) is reciprocal:

Doctor
: the *doctor* implicates his *mother's lover* in the theft of that love, the *lover,* the *doctor,* in the matter of the *first cousin.*

Doctor's first cousin
: the *first cousin* loves the *doctor* in love with his *mother,* who adores the *lover* seated next to the *cousin* whom he (the lover) loves.

Doctor's mother
: the *mother* fixes blame upon the *first cousin* for provocation of the *lover,* the *cousin* the *mother* for the preservation of the son's affection.

Doctor's mother's lover

Additional Data on the Doctor

His eyes are fierce enough to paralyze a legion.

He shares his father's residence in order to sustain the source of money and leisure necessary for the pursuit of pure melancholia.

He solicits followers, converts, fellow sufferers in silence. He gains them on balconies, under beds, in closets, where he has driven them from friends and relatives after his arrival.

He seeks a place where love is passed from one to another, but never returned: a solid formation of scowls, grimaces and frowns.

He prowls the rooms of sleeping bodies, running his hands over each, "Alert, arise, I've jumped the gates, guards, the sleeping dogs to find you; I've walked miles behind a cruising taxi—always a few kilometers ahead, testing its lights, horn, blaring radio music to accompany my pace. Finally it halted.

By the time I reached, the driver was slumped alseep in the back seat. I drove the rest of the way, parking across the street to confuse him. Up, before he starts off again."

For today the girls select puce/magenta against a grey/blue sky; for yesterday a celebration: sepia/pearl honoring a partial eclipse of the sun; tomorrow, ebony/coral — indigo/mauve? They ponder the scenery for pleasing harmonies of color. Bangles of lapis lazuli orbit their wrists: again and over, around and again, over and around. Their ears feel the flap of onyx earrings set in motion by the wind.

Each time the doctor disappears, they grieve. The two girls change to matching black. Children flee in terror to a distant playground. The mother bends forward and away in grief — if removed, would seem to occupy a rocking chair. The man and woman attend her motion.

(Various sound effects will be simulated: the recoil of a pistol, the friction of a fall, the last waver of a noosed one. . .)

During rains the two girls are perceived as peonies uprooted from the nonexistent window box. As soon as precipitation is felt merging with their bones, foresight borne from long exposure to the weather, they begin to scheme a blend of pink, red, and white.

He reappears, Huckleberry Finn arriving at his own funeral. He tiptoes from the elevator, is seated in the midst of his chairs — left, in his memory, as he had arranged them. A light veneer of dust has settled; he sneezes.

The two girls shed their black. The mother reactivates her pacing.

Each time he disappears, they will take up grieving—a diversion, a sabbatical, an outing, high adventure in their own house.

Those inside the room regard the girls as carefully tended fixtures. Until the day arrives, they will always block the window, shifting color only, producing like intervals of even modulated tones.

Behold!
in a one-room factory
THE VILLAGE BAKER

ensconced in the elements of his art, the art that shapes the bodies of the villagers.

His senses dissect the darkness: he hears the breathing of yeast buds, muffled under towels; he fingers the length of a wooden spoon — crafted to steer the convergence of flour and water; he discerns a villager crouched behind the oven door, intent on claiming the first warm loaf of the dawn.

• • •

I've seen them eat it. First they soften the loaf, stifling it between their hands, then fleshing it out; in and out, in and out, like an accordion. This brings forth a wheezing sound, barely audible, but in congregation — the background tone of their daily life. Next they reduce it to a flat circular form (much like that of a plate), throw back their heads, ingest, incorporate with a gulp.

• • •

Some feature crusts on their bodies. Wounds flourish underneath, seldom breaking to the surface. Those afflicted come to wield themselves as weapons — walking walls — threaten by leaning in any direction. Sometimes they strike while lost in reverie, oblivious to those passing by.

The soft doughy creatures seem to have escaped prematurely, before being shoveled from the oven. One demonstrated how he could probe from his ribs (which were limber) to his spinal cord without finding resistance. He requested a massive push from the back, however, after the completion of this feat, to restore his organs to their proper order.

Others have a brittle coating. Any collision with objects or with hands, even their own, produces a flaking. They take small quick steps, outpacing the long slow tread of the others; they vibrate with laughter squandering flakes like confetti around themselves. Living ghosts, they horrify the witness, able to pinpoint only a spattering of light when they speak.

25

• • •

Observe the children competing in the playground. They fling wads of dough in the air, then grapple, mouths agape, for the place on which the dough might fall.

Their teacher, the only spectator, does not join them on the field. He leans from a window, from the roof for an overview, falls into half sleep, gathering noise for clues. Finally he rings the school bells to drown it out.

He fails to understand — this alien imported from another locale, dependent on celery, bean sprouts, or spring onions for survival.

• • •

The bread creates its own audience, inducing a rising curve of craving. It deprives the villagers of the energy needed to set out for the fields each morning. Instead, they hire laborers, agents of the bakers who shield them from the concept of crop rotation — a means of coaxing the soil towards some alternative nutrient.

The bakers shun their own product as do their children and pets. In a bakery window—the one that follows the bent of the street—a pair of caged pigeons rustle, averting the focus of a glance. They yearn for egg yolks, in the apparent absence of bread crumbs.

• • •

en route to a bakery, I frequently falter . . . detour from the road for direction . . . the inhabitants, mouths occupied with bread, can provide only grunts . . . soon they are aligned on either side of the road, squinting in my direction as I pass beyond . . . suffering mass collisions of bread boxes in an effort to track this one-man procession

• • •

I mentioned that in Ecuador, the masses sculpt dolls from stale bread. The bread is modeled after those found in the vicinity of the sculptor — overseer, grandchildren, packmule or sometimes after the sculptor himself. The parts of the body are camouflaged in the colors of the surroundings and left to dry in the sun.

The dolls are then passed from hand to hand as gifts; to be laden with pelts or arranged behind opaque curtains, uncovered few times in any lifetime.

• • •

The baker pauses: eyes closed, tosses a loaf into the air, waits as the loaf gathers itself back together on the palms of his hands — each slice a child.

If our people possessed these instincts, he begins, they would model stale bread in the shape of fresh bread, then eat it. Furthermore, our bread is sold instantaneously — it rarely settles long enough to turn stale.

Even the dead are usually discovered before their loaves have grown stale. The remaining loaves are confiscated; the value deducted from funeral expenses. Before burial, one loaf is restored to the owner, inserted between his teeth. A donation of two rolls is also given—one to cover each eye.

• • •

Underground in shelter, parents suspect, the young break their boredom, apply jam, butter, or lard to their bread. Those wild creations of sound, the elation of infants, that pry the villagers from sleep — unable to locate the source, a spokesman suggests the wind, prodding them on towards home, "Tomorrow the annual parade may begin."

• • •

The participants have been selected for agility as well as wit. For months they have been absorbed in the making of their costumes. Now they are able to pass as replicas of the variety of bread they have chosen to represent. Skirmishes occur.

Of this first edition
there are 600 copies
of which 100 are hard-covers
numbered and signed by the author.